MOZART
The Man Behind the Music

The life and times of Wolfgang Amadeus Mozart – a literary picture book

DONOVAN BIXLEY

upstart press

Germani

Groningen · Bremen · Oldenburg · Hamburg · Zeven · Norderstedt · Lübeck · Schwerin · Neubrandenburg · Prikzwalk · BERLIN · Growzów · Koszalin · Piła · Gdańsk · Elbląg · Bialystok · Stettin · Bydgoszcz · Olsztyn

Dortmund · Düsseldorf · Hannover · Wolfsburg · Magdeburg · Potsdam · Zielonia Góra · Poznań · Płock · Warsaw · Radom · Lu

Rhein · Cologne · Göttingen · Gotha · Halle · Leipzig · Cottbus · Dresden · Liberec · Kalisz · Łódź · Wrocław · Kielce · Kraków

Strasbourg · Bonn · Frankfurt · Erfurt · Bamberg · Karlovy Vary · Wałbrzych · Bielsko-Biala · Metz

MANNHEIM · Heidelberg · Nürnberg · Plzeň · PRAGUE · Beroun · Jihlava · Brno · Trenčín

Karlsruhe · Stuttgart · R. Danube · Budějovice · Zitersdorf · VIENNA · Banská · Gyor · Budapest

AUGSBURG · Landshut · Passau · SALZBURG · Baden · Bratislava · Veszprém · Kaposvár

Schwabmünchen · MÜNCHEN · Hallein · Linz · Graz

Innsbruck · Wörgl · Klagenfurt · Maribor · Hungaria

Helvetia · Zurich · Bolzano · Trento · Vicenza · Treviso · Ljubljana · Zagreb · Tuzla

Geneve · Bergamo · Roverto · Venice · Pula · Rijeka · Banja Luka · Sarajevo · Belgrade

MILAN · Brescia · Verona · Mantua · Zadar · Split · Metko

Turin · Asti · Genoa · Parma · Italia · Ravenna · Rimini · Dubrovnik

Savona · Nice · BOLOGNA · Pisa · Adriatic Sea · Podgorica · Albas

Ligurian Sea · FLORENCE · R. Arno · Viterbo · Cassino · Podgorica · Skopi

Corsica · Tyrrhenian Sea · R. Tiber · Grosseto · San Severo · Campobasso · Andria · Foggia · Tirana

Ajaccio · ROME · Latina · Cassino · Bari · Vlorë · Bitola

Sassari · NAPLES · Salerno · Potenza · Taranto

Scale
Mill: Germani
0   10   20   30   40

Wolfgang Amadeus Mozart

is a name forever linked with musical genius.

He really was a genuine sensation, and his music has become such a part of our culture that it's as recognisable as a nursery rhyme. If you've heard only one piece of classical music, it's likely to be Mozart. He was the hero of Tchaikovsky and remains a perennial favourite of orchestras across the world, heard everywhere from cafés to Hollywood action blockbusters. But the musical legacy and the Mozart myth often overshadow the incredible life which formed his genius.

Mozart was so much more than just the archetypal child prodigy. He became one of the great social change-makers of his era, from his socially challenging operas to stamping his mark on the world as a ground-breaking freelance artist. We know all this because Mozart's father, Leopold, saved hundreds of family letters dating from Mozart's childhood through to his early thirties.

Mozart's grammar and spelling are quite erratic, and his punctuation is practically non-existent. Some of the quotes in this book have been adapted and abridged to make them more readable, whilst still retaining the spirit and meaning of Mozart's originals.

Mozart's letters reveal his brushes with the great and the powerful, as well as his development from miniature trickster to one of the greatest composers of all time. But achieving success was an endless struggle. It took decades

of tireless work and constant battles with jealous rivals, the aristocracy and even his own family.

What makes Mozart so inspiring is his incredible self-belief in the face of such adversity. He had an indomitable perky personality, and at every setback he would pick himself up and re-double his efforts. That human quality shines through Mozart's music and still touches us, centuries after his death.

This book offers a peek through the keyhole at Mozart's world. Not the genius alone in his ivory tower, but a real man who lived a real life — the cheeky little brother, the rebellious son, the besotted young lover, the arrogant artist, the despondent freelancer, the proud father and the doting husband.

So what about the legends that surround Mozart? Did he really have an uncontrollable fear of the trumpet? Was he actually engaged to his sweaty, overweight piano pupil? And what did he say about Beethoven behind his back? Read on and discover the man behind the music.

♪ A soundtrack for the music listed in this book
is available on Spotify: "Faithfully Mozart".

I cannot write poetically,
for I am no poet. I cannot arrange
my words so artfully that they reflect
shadow and light, for I am no painter …
But I can do it with the sounds of music;
for I am a composer.

WOLFGANG

The miracle which God let be born in Salzburg.

LEOPOLD MOZART ABOUT WOLFGANG

Little Wolfgang must have seemed a kind of personal miracle to his parents when he was born in Salzburg on 27 January 1756. Johannes Chrysostomus Wolfgangus Theophilus Mozart (to give him his full name) was only the second of Leopold and Anna Maria's seven children to survive, but he soon proved to be someone quite extraordinary to the wider world as well. When Wolfgang's older sister, Maria Anna, nicknamed Nannerl, began harpsichord lessons at the age of eight, four-year-old Wolfgang joined in, enthusiastically teaching himself from her lesson book. But what really astounded their papa, Leopold, was that only one year later little "Wolferl" began to write down his own compositions♪. Leopold knew his son was very special, and would soon promote him to the world as a miracle from God.

♪ ANDANTE IN C FOR PIANO, K. 1A

Everyone is amazed, especially at the boy, and everyone whom I have heard says that his genius is incomprehensible.

LEOPOLD MOZART

The word "genius" is bandied around so freely these days, but there were many factors which formed Wolfgang into one of history's true geniuses, not least of all his intense passion for music. His sister said that it was impossible to get her young brother off the keyboard before midnight, and he worked so tirelessly that he needed no practice after the age of seven. But talent alone was not enough. It was essential that Wolfgang was born at the right time in history — when music was the reigning art form — and in the right place, central to the musical capitals of Europe. Importantly, their father (and teacher) was able to pass on everything he knew. Leopold Mozart was a violinist and composer, who had published a successful book on violin method in the year of Wolfgang's birth. The unique factor was Wolfgang's ridiculous physical ability. For a pre-schooler to master the harpsichord, his fine motor skills and hand-eye co-ordination must have been almost incomprehensible.

Their Majesties received us with such extraordinary graciousness … Suffice to say that Wolferl jumped up on the Empress's lap, put his arms around her neck and kissed her heartily.

LEOPOLD MOZART

Musical prodigies were not uncommon in Mozart's era, and the standard procedure was to cash in before the novelty wore off. Both Wolfgang and Nannerl were remarkable musicians, so in 1762, Leopold took his family on tour, first to perform in Munich, then to Vienna, where they were invited to perform at the Imperial Palace. Wolfgang was such an exuberant six-year-old, winning friends wherever the family travelled. On entering Vienna, they were let off paying customs when Wolfgang played his violin for the official. At Schönbrunn Palace he proposed marriage to the young Archduchess — the future Queen of France, Marie Antoinette. Crowds turned out to see these curiosities run through their musical tricks — sight-reading anything placed before them, and playing with the keyboard hidden under a cloth. The Empress Maria Theresa gifted Wolfgang and Nannerl some exquisite clothes, and a chuffed Leopold had their portraits painted.

Musician friends came and went at the Mozart household. Court trumpeter and family friend, Johann Schachtner, was visiting when, to everyone's astonishment, seven-year-old Wolfgang simply picked up a violin and joined in with the adults without any practice. Schachtner recalled that once Wolfgang discovered music, his senses were dead to all other amusements unless they were accompanied by music too. However, little Wolferl had no love for the trumpet. Years later, he would still refer disparagingly to "trumpeters and their tricks" — perhaps as a result of a mean experiment played on him by Papa and Schachtner.

If anyone so much as showed him a trumpet it was like holding a loaded pistol to his heart. His father wished to rid him of this childish fear and ordered me to blow a trumpet at him regardless.

JOHANN ANDREAS SCHACHTNER

A person remains a poor creature without travel.

WOLFGANG

Wolfgang would spend almost a third of his life on the road and his first big adventure started in 1763. After the successful performances in Munich and Vienna, Leopold took the whole family on a grand tour of Europe that would last three and a half years.

There was more than financial benefits for the young Mozart. As well as brushing shoulders with the rich and the royal, it was tremendously important in Wolfgang's development to learn from the greatest composers, singers and musicians of the era. Leopold wrote, "What he knew when we left Salzburg is a mere shadow of what he knows now." In London, the eight-year-old was inspired to write his first symphony after performing with Johann Christian Bach — he even contemplated writing an opera!

During these years on tour, Leopold turned all his energies to Wolfgang, all but ignoring his daughter. Perhaps it was simply commercial. Wolfgang was very small for his age and drew bigger crowds for more years, often because Leopold exaggerated Wolfgang's youth. That kind of behaviour got Leopold offside with the aristocracy. In London he put on a cheap tavern show after the aristocracy had already paid top dollar to see Wolfgang play. News of the Mozarts' money-grubbing quickly spread amongst Europe's nobility. Unfortunately this would have consequences throughout Wolfgang's life, when it came to looking for a position at court.

At the age of thirteen, it was time for Wolfgang to shake the tag of "child prodigy" and make that difficult transition to serious composer. To complete his musical education, he and Papa headed to Italy, but on this tour, his sister had to stay at home with Mama. At eighteen, Nannerl was no longer considered a curiosity.

Wolfgang's earliest surviving letters reveal the young genius to be a typical teenage boy, who liked fast coaches and was always sleepy.

I feel so jolly on this trip, because it's so cosy in our carriage, and because our coachman is a fine fellow who drives as fast as he can when the road gives him the slightest chance.

WOLFGANG

Wolfgang's teenage letters from Italy are filled with self-deprecating jokes and multi-language puns. He calls himself "simple Simon", "dope", "booby", "dunce" and "numbskull". Yet young Wolfgang was no dope. He had learnt Italian (the language of music) from Papa and the court musicians in Salzburg. He also became fluent in French and Latin, as well as having a smattering of English.

The purpose of the journey was to complete Wolfgang's musical education as a composer, and Italy was the home of European music. Here, for the first time, Wolfgang substituted the Italian "Amadeo" for his middle name, Theophilus, meaning "beloved of God". In later years he frequently used the French "Amadé", but he rarely used the well-known "Amadeus" (from Latin). It appears only a handful of times in his surviving correspondence.

I remain … the same old buffoon, Wolfgang in Germania, Amadeo in Italia De Mozartini

WOLFGANG

Wolfgang was constantly absorbing Italian music, especially opera. He was surrounded by the most famous singers and composers, and met the most powerful rulers in Italy. But along with his serious devotion to music, Wolfgang showed an early aptitude for human observation — a perfect trait for a future opera composer. In fact, the characters from his letters seem as if they have stepped straight off the stage in a comic opera, with gluttonous priests stuffing their faces and whining prima donnas who don't open their mouths when they sing. In Verona, a ballet performed with the opera really tickled Wolfgang's funny bone.

A grotesco dancer was at the opera;
he let out a fart each time he jumped.

WOLFGANG

In Florence, Wolfgang met a kindred spirit, the violinist Thomas Linley — "a young Englishman … who plays absolutely beautifully," Leopold wrote home. The two young prodigies were both fourteen, and had great fun outdoing each other on their violins. Linley was studying under the famous violinist Pietro Nardini, and would become known as "The English Mozart". Wolfgang later said that Linley was a true genius and "would have been one of the greatest ornaments of the musical world". Tragically it was not to be, as Linley drowned in a boating accident when he was just twenty-two.

The two boys performed one after the other all evening, constantly embracing each other.

LEOPOLD MOZART

By April 1770, Wolfgang and Leopold had travelled through Italy to Rome. At the Vatican they were mistaken for a German prince and his tutor — much to Wolfgang's delight. In the Sistine Chapel, beneath Michelangelo's glorious ceiling, they heard Gregorio Allegri's *Miserere*. This sacred piece of music was kept under lock and key, and copying it was forbidden by pain of excommunication. Wolfgang went back to their lodgings and wrote down the whole score from memory after hearing it just once! Leopold boasted about this legendary feat, but Wolfgang simply joked about having to share a bed with Papa and made fun of visiting the Vatican, where the faithful and tourists kiss the foot of St Peter's statue.

I have had the honour of kissing
St Peter's foot … and as I have the
misfortune to be so small, I, that same
old numbskull, Wolfgang Mozart,
had to be lifted up.

WOLFGANG

Wolfgang and Leopold continued their tour down to Naples. They went sightseeing at Vesuvius, and Wolfgang reported that the volcano was "really letting off smoke today". Throughout his life Wolfgang was much more interested in people, and rarely described his surroundings. Humour was at the forefront of his mind, and a sighting of the king at the Naples opera house gave Wolfgang good material.

The king is a crude Neapolitan, and in the opera house he always stands on a little stool so as to look a little taller than the Queen.

WOLFGANG

I have the honour of being your very humble servant, Chevalier de Mozart

WOLFGANG

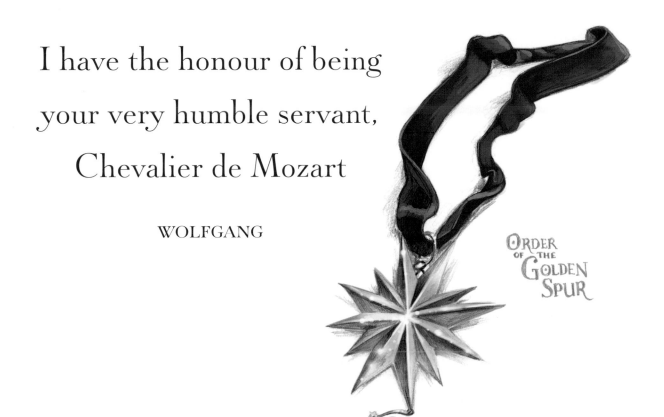

ORDER OF THE GOLDEN SPUR

On returning to Rome, Pope Clement XIV bestowed the Order of the Golden Spur on Wolfgang. He was given a golden cross on a red sash, along with a sword and spurs. The fourteen year old was now a knight, permitted to title himself "Chevalier" and carry a sword in public.

More honours awaited in Bologna, where Wolfgang became the youngest composer to be admitted into the Accademia Filarmonica, Bologna's famous society of maestros. Wolfgang was locked in a room and set a composition exam, which he completed in half the time of many older composers. However, it is quite likely that Wolfgang was given a sneak preview of the exam. Nonetheless, the young maestro was about to be given a *true* test of his skills — he'd been commissioned to write a full opera for the Milan opera house.

Wolfgang had already whipped out four Italian symphonies on his travels, but now the teenager was entrusted to write an opera for Milan. *Mithridates, King of Pontus* premiered on Boxing Day 1770, with Wolfgang conducting from the harpsichord. He wore a red coat with blue trim, tailored especially for the opening, and it was a real thrill for him when the music-loving Milanese called him "Il Signor Cavaliere Filarmonico" — appreciating his great honours received in Rome and Bologna. The Mozarts were paid 450 gulden, a whole year's salary back in Salzburg, and they celebrated the successful premiere with Wolfgang's favourite meal, liver dumplings and sauerkraut. The opera, a massive undertaking, had been written in just two months! Along the way, Wolfgang and Papa had been constantly on edge. They had encountered jealous and obstructive orchestra members and prima donnas who had tried to trip up the young maestro. By the end of it all, Wolfgang was completely exhausted.

I'm getting sleepy, and
Papa said just now, "Then stop writing"
… Wolfgang Mozart, whose fingers are
tired, tired, tired, tired, from writing.

WOLFGANG

Wolfgang turned fifteen in January 1771. He and Papa had now been away from Salzburg for over a year. On their return home, they stopped in Venice, where they were hosted by a Salzburg family now living in the city. Their days were spent cruising up and down the Grand Canal and performing at the noble houses. Wolfgang was charmed by Venice, in fact he was in heaven, being chased about by the six daughters of his host family as they tried to give him "the treatment".

"The treatment" … is to have your bottom bumped against the floor, to make you a true Venetian … all the women got together and attacked me.

WOLFGANG

Before they had even returned to Salzburg, Leopold and Wolfgang received a new commission — an opera for Archduke Ferdinand's marriage, which was to take place in Milan in October 1771. So, after only a few months at home with Mama and Nannerl, maestro and father were back on the road to Italy.

Wolfgang's mind was swirling with the serious task of composing an opera. Their accommodations were packed with orchestra members, and Wolfgang was inspired by all the sounds drifting from the apartments. "It's such fun for composing," he wrote to his sister. He was constantly tired and hardly had time for his usual humorous observations. With years of touring under his belt, he'd become quite the seasoned traveller.

I saw four fellows hanged
here in the Piazza del Duomo.
They hang them just as they do in Lyon.

WOLFGANG

Wolfgang and Papa had one more trip to Milan in late 1772. Wolfgang's opera, *Lucio Silla*, was an inspired fresh work, and a fabulous success to boot. It was now that Wolfgang wrote one of his first masterpieces, *Exsultate, jubilate♪*. During the Italian tours the hope had always been to secure Wolfgang a full-time position at court. Leopold believed that they were certain to get a post. They had tried many times before, but now Wolfgang was no longer a child, he was a bona fide applauded and seasoned maestro — surely things had changed? The Mozarts would have been horrified if they knew what the aristocracy *really* thought of them. When seventeen-year-old Archduke Ferdinand asked his mother if he should employ the Mozarts, the Empress responded with harsh advice …

You are requesting that I take the young Salzburger into your service. I don't know that you would need a composer … what I am saying is to prevent you from being burdened with useless people and give titles to them … when they are going around the world like beggars.

EMPRESS MARIA THERESA

The three Italian tours had made the Mozarts quite comfortable. In September 1773, they moved out of Wolfgang's tiny birth-house, in the heart of Salzburg's old town, to a spacious new home across the river, which had been a dance studio. Earlier in the year, Wolfgang and Leopold had taken another job-seeking trip to Vienna, oblivious to the aristocracy's disdain. "The empress was very gracious," reported Leopold. "But that was all." It was not a completely wasted journey, though. Wolfgang was now steeped in the lyrical music of Italy, and in Vienna he discovered the powerful music of Joseph Haydn. On returning home, Wolfgang immediately wrote one of his greatest early masterpieces, his "little" G minor symphony♪.

Settling back in Salzburg was a massive come down for Wolfgang, after the years of touring Europe's greatest cities. To make matters worse, fortunes had changed at home — Salzburg had a new lord, the Prince-Archbishop Colloredo. Wolfgang had been appointed a permanent paid position in the court orchestra; however, where their previous lord had indifferently accommodated their comings and goings, Colloredo was intent on putting the Mozarts in their place. That place was *not* as gallivanting maestros but as servants, there to do their lord's bidding. From now on Leopold and Wolfgang had to grovel and beg for every favour. Wolfgang's ego had been well fed in Italy, and now the seventeen-year-old saw his hopes and dreams slipping away. He started to resent the confines of his small home town, and the new Archbishop Colloredo. It wasn't long before these two stubborn personalities began butting heads.

I have nothing to hope for in Salzburg and would do better to seek my fortune elsewhere.

WOLFGANG

My opera was performed yesterday … the theatre was so packed that a great many people were turned away … it feels so good to breathe away from Salzburg.

WOLFGANG

Wolfgang had been mouldering away in Salzburg for a couple of years when he was given a gasp of fresh air. He was commissioned to write a comedy opera — this time for the Munich opera house. *La Finta Giardiniera* (The Pretend Garden-Girl) premiered on 13 January 1775. It was not a huge success, but nonetheless Wolfgang was invigorated to be in Munich, celebrating the carnival season with "all the pretty girls here". It was only a brief respite from the Archbishop, and soon Wolfgang was back in Salzburg, where he would stay for another two years. His mind was still swirling with ideas for operas and he produced an innovative violin concerto♪ where the soloist enters with a different theme from the main orchestra, similar to the way an opera diva enters with her own tune.

My chief reason for detesting Salzburg
is the coarse, slovenly, run-down
court orchestra. No man with any
self-respect can live with such musicians.

WOLFGANG

Wolfgang was a serious composer and his gripes extended to court organist Michael Haydn (younger brother of Joseph) who performed whilst drunk. Still, Wolfgang continued to produce challenging works. For New Year 1777 he composed his Serenade No. 8♪, a quadraphonic extravaganza for four orchestras. The piece was written to create a delightful echo effect … if only Wolfgang could get those slovenly musicians into shape.

Father and son have my permission to seek their fortunes elsewhere.

ARCHBISHOP COLLOREDO

After many years of tensions between the Mozarts and their lord, the Prince-Archbishop Colloredo, Wolfgang had finally had enough. In August 1777, he asked permission to travel and seek an appointment at a more worthy court — hopefully in Southern Germany, where the rest of the family could join him. Colloredo responded with a letter that sounded terribly like a dismissal for *both* father and son. So … Leopold, ever cautious, decided to remain employed, while Wolfgang prepared to set off in search of his fortune.

So began Wolfgang's long hard journey to independence. This time Papa stayed at home with Nannerl, while Mama headed off with Wolfgang in their new coach. The twenty-one-year-old felt "as light as a feather" to finally be out from under the archbishop's thumb — *he* was the prince now. Papa was still a dominating figure, controlling operations from home, and Wolfgang was keen to show that he was equal to the task. On 23 September 1777, they stopped on their first night towards bigger and better things. Wolfgang was *trying* to be responsible and serious — but that wasn't going to last long.

I am the second Papa now.
I'm taking care of everything ...
I'm sitting here like a prince.

WOLFGANG

Leopold had always been Wolfgang's faithful companion, organising every detail and supplying full descriptions of every event. Mama, on the other hand, shared a wicked sense of humour with her son. In one letter she tells Leopold to "stay well in body and mind / and try to kiss your own behind" — as well as many ruder limericks. It's easy to picture Anna Maria and Wolfgang as a jolly party on their first stop at the Court of the Electorate of Bavaria in Munich. Mother and son were full of high hopes and Wolfgang's immediate writing style reflects his hilarious mood — as if we are there in the room with him.

I have hardly written 10 words when I hear something … it smells like something burning … Then Mama says to me: I bet you let one off?

WOLFGANG

Bring on the best composers from Munich …
Italy and France, Germany, England, and Spain.
I am willing to be tested against any of them.

WOLFGANG

Wolfgang wasn't short on confidence and his résumé *was* impressive. All of which made it even more frustrating when Munich's court lackeys did their best to keep him from seeing His Highness The Elector. Wolfgang had effectively walked out on his Salzburg master, naïvely unaware that he was not going to be offered a position at any of the neighbouring courts. There was no chance of the nobility taking Mozart's side in an argument with Salzburg's powerful Prince-Archbishop Colloredo. It wasn't long before Wolfgang and Mama were sent packing.

After getting the cold shoulder in Munich, Wolfgang and Mama headed on to Augsburg, Leopold's home town in Bavaria. Wolfgang was shown around by the magistrate's son, and his boorish brother-in-law, including a visit to the famous piano maker, Johann Stein. Just that year, Stein had invented the first pianoforte with a release-action hammer and a knee-operated sustain — the precursor to the modern piano and an instrument which Wolfgang would go on to make his own. Wolfgang was in a playful mood, trying to keep his identity a surprise. He handed the besotted Stein a letter of introduction then leapt on the nearest instrument to let his playing reveal his identity.

Stein shook his head, and said finally:
"Is it possible I have the honour of seeing Herr Mozart before me?"
"Oh no," I replied. "My name is Trazom."

WOLFGANG

I prefer Stein's claviers … what distinguishes his instruments from all others is that they are built with an escapement … without escapement action it is impossible to play a piano forte and not produce a clangy and vibrating after-effect.

WOLFGANG

Wolfgang loved playing on Stein's claviers, and gave a concert in Augsburg performing some of his old piano sonatas♪. He gives us a comparison between this brand-new instrument and the clangy, vibrating old harpsichord. Wolfgang's letters put you next to him at the clavier, and he gives us a sense of the type of tricks he performed at parties. What's interesting is that Wolfgang uses very child-like, non-musical language. Despite being one of the greatest musical geniuses, he disdained high-brow musical jargon. Instead, music was a living thing, something to be pranced about the room, or taken for a little stroll.

I asked him to give me a theme …
I took the theme for a walk, then in the middle — the theme was in G minor — I changed it to major … then I played it again, but this time assbackwards.

WOLFGANG

Papa was keen for Wolfgang to make a grand impression in Augsburg. He insisted that Wolfgang wear his medallion of the Golden Spur, a true honour indeed, which entitled Wolfgang to call himself Chevalier and carry a sword. It was not a persona Wolfgang craved, but nevertheless he obeyed Papa and went out on the town with the magistrate's "foppish son" and friends. Unfortunately the star-encircled cross of the medallion drew rather the opposite desired effect. Wolfgang reported their mocking comments in a bitter letter home to Papa. After taking their insults all evening, Wolfgang snatched up his sword and hat, fuming: "It would be easier for me to obtain all the orders which it is possible to win than for you to become what I am, even if you were to die twice and be born again."

They kept addressing me repeatedly: "Hallo, you fine gentleman, Knight of the Spur … How much does it cost? … Does one need permission to wear it? … Let's all send away for our crosses."

WOLFGANG

Wolfgang and Mama left Augsburg in a cloud of frustration, arriving in Mannheim on 30 October 1777. Despite the setbacks in Munich and Augsburg, Wolfgang was still feeling cocky and confident. For a start, the city starred the finest orchestra in all of Europe. Wolfgang abandoned trivial aspirations as a mere performer. He was to be a great maestro, and immediately set about securing the top job of kapellmeister — the musical director at court.

I am a composer, and I was born to be a kapellmeister. I must not and will not bury my gift for composing, which God in his goodness has so richly endowed me.

WOLFGANG

The presence of a young genius at court made many of the musicians defensive of their hard won positions. It was not helped that Wolfgang was adept at ruffling feathers with his frank opinions. A particular target of his mockery was Mannheim's deputy director of the orchestra, Georg Joseph Vogler. "Vogler is a fool," Wolfgang wrote to his father — thinking he could easily take Vogler's job through talent alone. Unsurprisingly, Vogler worked behind the scenes to make sure Wolfgang would never be offered *any* position.

Briefly, I hear an idea which is not at all bad — well it will certainly not remain *not at all bad* for long. It will soon become *dreadfully* bad.

WOLFGANG ON HEARING VOGLER'S MUSIC

Payment for performing had always been a problem for the Mozarts. "What one needs on a journey is cash," Wolfgang reported from Mannheim. Things *seemed* to get off to a good start, with Wolfgang giving two concerts for His Highness, The Elector. Now, at the age of twenty-one, Wolfgang wanted to be accepted as a serious composer, demanding a proper salary — not the trinkets and snuff boxes he'd received as a child. But it seemed that old habits die hard. "I now own five watches," wrote Wolfgang, in a highly sarcastic mode.

As I expected. No money, but a fine gold watch … I am seriously thinking of having extra watch pockets sewn on my trousers, so when I visit some great lord … it will not occur to him to present me with another one.

WOLFGANG

I, Johannes Chrysostomus Amadeus Wolfgangus Sigismundus Mozart, confess to not coming home until 12 o'clock midnight … I did some rhymes about crude stuff, such as muck, shitting, and ass licking … I must confess too, that I thoroughly enjoyed it.

WOLFGANG

Wolfgang made fast friends with a lively bunch from the Mannheim court orchestra. We get a glimpse of the very sociable fellow, who loved performing at parties and had a natural talent at making up lewd rhymes. He was thoroughly enjoying his new-found freedom, as demonstrated in this mock confession to his father. Papa was less than impressed, inquiring how often Wolfgang was going to confession and commenting on his son's newly grown stubble. But Wolfgang was having the time of his life. In fact, he'd only just got started. He was about to drop some news that would send Leopold into a tailspin.

Is Wolfgang's beard going to be cut off,
singed off, or maybe even shaved off?

LEOPOLD MOZART

I firmly resolve to go on with
the sinful life which I have begun …
because the play must go on.

WOLFGANG

I recommend the poor, but virtuous, Mademoiselle Weber with all my heart.

WOLFGANG

Love was in the air. By the start of 1778, Wolfgang was besotted with one of his pupils, sixteen-year-old singer Aloysia Weber. The Webers would play an important part in Wolfgang's life, and he had taken pity on the struggling family, which included younger sisters Constanze and Sophie. However, Leopold had mortgaged himself to the hilt so that Wolfgang could find a well-paying position. Papa had no intention of adding a strange family to his debts, and he tried to put Wolfgang off with subtle arguments. This only spurred Wolfgang to leap to Aloysia's defence.

There are people who think that no one can love a poor girl without having evil designs.

WOLFGANG

The aria I wrote for Mademoiselle Weber … was written solely for her and fits her like a well-tailored garment.

WOLFGANG

On the journey so far, Wolfgang had shown he was rather susceptible to flattery, and easily influenced by others, when they were actually working against him. Falling in love for the first time, he really drifts off into la-la land — planning trips to Italy with Aloysia and imagining them as a dream couple, with Aloysia as a prima donna and Wolfgang as the famous composer. In contrast to his sarcastic mocking side, we now see a very giving young man who puts everything else aside, writing Aloysia an aria specifically to showcase her talent♪. Sure enough, she benefited tremendously from Wolfgang's experience and would soon become one of the great singers of her time.

♪'ALCANDRO, LO CONFESSO', K. 294

Leopold was beside himself, and tried to regain control of his son, reminding Wolfgang forcefully of the family's "present situation". Repaying debt by getting a permanent court position was the real purpose of the trip! Below, Leopold paints Wolfgang's dreams into a very bleak nightmare. But Wolfgang was gaining more confidence in his independence, and he was not so easily put off.

It now depends on you alone to raise yourself to a position of eminence, such as no musician has ever obtained … of whom posterity will read … or to die bedded on straw in an attic full of starving children.

LEOPOLD MOZART

Wolfgang dilly-dallied in Mannheim for month after month, wooing Aloysia and hoping to persuade Papa of her virtues. Leopold was tearing his hair out. His letters became more and more insistent and agitated, listing point by point recriminations against Wolfgang — accusing his son of frittering away the family's savings and putting another family above his own. Wolfgang's sister had even poured her own life savings into the venture. Years later, Nannerl bitterly held on to the belief that her little brother was hopeless with money and remained more or less a child, with his head in the clouds. Wolfgang was eventually brought crashing down to earth when Leopold wrote:

I look like poor Lazarus. My coat is in tatters … my old flannel vest is so torn that I can hardly keep it on any longer.

LEOPOLD MOZART

The whole incident sparked a real split between Wolfgang and his father and sister. Leopold was literally broke, whilst Wolfgang was broken-hearted at the thought of leaving Aloysia. As winter set in, Wolfgang stayed inside, barely able to scratch a few lines to Papa. In contrast to his previous boasts of being a born kapellmeister, our great genius now has doubts — playing down his talents as a mere wood tapper.

I shall prostitute myself and ask if they want me to bang out something on the piano … after all, I am a born wood tapper who can do nothing but bash the piano a little!

WOLFGANG

I have now set all my hopes

on Paris, for the German princes

are all penny-pinchers.

WOLFGANG

By March 1778, Wolfgang and Mama had run out of ready cash. They borrowed even more money to travel on to France, where they had to sell their coach to their driver. Wolfgang found travelling tedious at the best of times, and he was in a surly mood as they headed to Paris. Anna Maria was supposed to return to Salzburg, but chose instead to travel on and keep Wolfgang company. It was a decision that would prove to have a fateful and dramatic effect on Wolfgang's life.

After being on the road for 9½ days …

I have never been so bored in my life.

WOLFGANG

The distances here are too great for walking — or the roads too muddy — for the mud in Paris is beyond all description.

WOLFGANG

In April 1778, Wolfgang set about making contacts in Paris. Leopold had given him a long list of friends who had helped the family on their visit to the French capital fifteen years previously. But Wolfgang was in a rude frame of mind, desperately pining for Aloysia in Mannheim. It muddied his impressions and left him with an instant dislike of everything Parisian.

The French are not nearly so polite as they were 15 years ago; their manners now border on rudeness.

WOLFGANG

I sit alone in my room all day long as if I were in prison … With great difficulty I manage to knit a little by the daylight that struggles in.

ANNA MARIA MOZART

The first weeks in Paris were a difficult time for both mother and son. Anna Maria did not speak French and whiled away her days in their apartment. In a sad letter to Leopold, she complained that the room was too small for a piano, so Wolfgang was rarely at home. Wolfgang hoped for important introductions from Baron Friedrich Melchior von Grimm, a friend who had helped the Mozarts fifteen years earlier. Unfortunately, the Baron's objective criticism rubbed raw against Wolfgang's spiky mood.

To make his fortune I wish he
had half the talent and
twice as much cunning.

BARON VON GRIMM ON WOLFGANG

I see a crowd of miserable bunglers
making a living here, and with my
talents, should I not be able to do so?

WOLFGANG

In no time, Wolfgang inadvertently insulted everyone in the Parisian music scene — their singers mangled Italian, their composers were tired old hacks, and even their language was an "invention of the Devil". After the rapturous receptions he'd had in Mannheim, Wolfgang didn't take kindly to being relegated to second fiddle. At one aristocratic house he was forced to wait in an ice-cold room then was made to play background music, whilst his hosts threw open the shutters and sketched Paris.

What really annoyed me was
that Madame and all her gentlemen
never interrupted their drawing for
a moment … and I was left to play
for the chairs, tables and walls.

WOLFGANG

I tremble from head to foot with eagerness to teach these French more thoroughly how to appreciate the Germans.

WOLFGANG

The French had no time for a former child prodigy. They were caught up in the argument over who was the greatest opera composer — the German Christoph Willibald Gluck or the Italian Niccolò Piccinni. "I'll thank God if I come out of here with my taste still intact," Wolfgang bristled. But, after many misunderstandings, and the mysterious disappearance of one of his compositions, things were about to get better. Wolfgang landed a commission to write a grand symphony. He was regaining that cocky swagger, and he was going to show the French *just* what he could do.

I decided … if my symphony went as badly as it did at the rehearsal, I would certainly make my way into the orchestra … and conduct myself!

WOLFGANG

Wolfgang was always in his element when he had work to do. Now he demonstrated the versatility of his genius by assimilating the French style in a matter of weeks. His new symphony♪ needed to please the unique tastes of the Parisians, and he started it with a special bang to make them sit up and listen. Self-doubt was gone, and even when the dress rehearsal ended in an utter shambles, the old Wolfgang was back and taking control — ready for the first performance on 18 June 1778. With it, the London papers would soon proclaim him among Europe's top composers.

The whole audience was sent into raptures … I was so pleased, I went right after the symphony to the Palace Royale and bought myself an ice-cream.

WOLFGANG

Wolfgang's "Paris" symphony was an instant hit, and its success was reported widely. Things were definitely looking up for mother and son — glorious summer had arrived and they had moved into a sunny new apartment. Anna Maria was even getting out and about. Around the time of Wolfgang's symphony, she visited the art galleries, and laughed that people back home would stare and gape at the fashions in Paris. Ominously, her last letter mentions feeling "strangely tired".

Mourn with me …
This has been the saddest day of my life
… my dear mother is no more! …
I pressed her hand and spoke to her —
but she did not see me, did not hear me
… she died five hours later.

WOLFGANG

On 3 July 1778, Wolfgang wrote to his father: "I have to bring you some very distressing and sad news … my dear mother is very ill." As Wolfgang described her sudden turn for the worse, he was actually hiding an awful secret — Mama had already died. Alone, at two o'clock in the morning, he struggled to find the right words to tell Papa and Nannerl, far away in Salzburg. Wolfgang revealed the terrible truth in a letter to a family friend, asking them to prepare his father and sister for the worst.

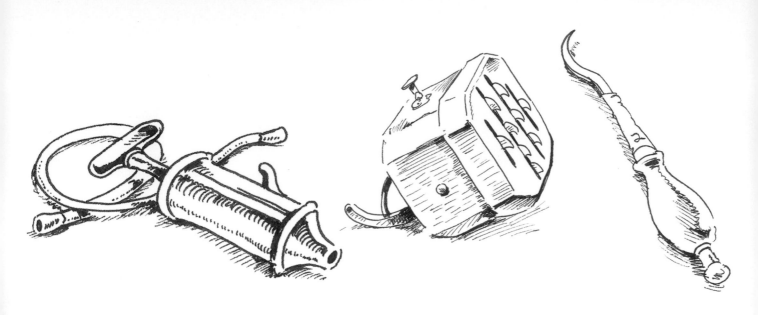

I have never seen anyone die, although I have often wished to. How cruel that my first experience should be the death of my mother!

WOLFGANG

Leopold knew his son well and instantly recognised Wolfgang's attempts to hide a darker truth. He demanded a blow-by-blow account of the events leading up to his wife's death. Their correspondence is remarkably matter-of-fact and gives us a curious insight into the world of eighteenth-century medicine and the treatments which probably hastened Anna Maria's demise. Wolfgang writes that Mama didn't want to have an enema, which was the fashion in Paris. Instead, she would only see a German doctor, who then prescribed rhubarb powder and wine and, of course, bleeding.

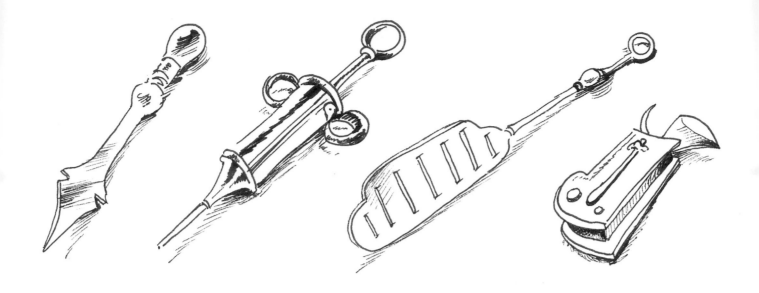

I cannot tell you accurately how much
she was bled, for here, it is measured not
by the ounce but by the plate — and she
was bled almost two platefuls.

WOLFGANG

Anna Maria Mozart was buried the day after her death, on 4 July 1778, at the cemetery of Saint Eustache in Paris. The cause of death is unknown, but it is possible she died of louse-borne typhus.

Understandably, Wolfgang was an emotional wreck after the death of his mother, and his state of mind was not eased by his financial problems. Wolfgang had written a sublime flute and harp concerto♪ for the Duke de Guines and his daughter, but getting these aristocrats to part with some of their riches took weeks and weeks. Paris was at the height of aristocratic privilege and decadence, and Wolfgang was rightly infuriated when the housekeeper finally took pity on him and paid him out of her *own purse* — although, only for his lessons and not the concerto. "Now there's noble treatment for you!" Wolfgang seethed.

It was a period of swinging emotions for Wolfgang. Paris was unbearable, but Salzburg was worse. He hated the aristocracy, but he wanted them to give him a job. Lastly, he was still head over heels in love with Aloysia, but now he was unsure if *she* still loved him.

We are not aristocrats …

we carry our riches in our brains, and

these no one can take from us, unless

they chop off our heads.

WOLFGANG

Papa tried to bring his son home, but Wolfgang convinced his father that Paris was a city of riches if you just kept your head about it. He'd actually been offered the job of organist at the Palace of Versailles and the pay was twice his salary back in Salzburg, for working only six months of the year. Wolfgang argued that the money hardly covered living in Europe's most expensive city, and he turned the job down — perhaps a fortunate decision given the bloody revolution that was brewing in France. The sad truth was that, since the death of Mama, Wolfgang's wealth of creativity had practically dried up.

Wolfgang faffed about in Paris for another three months, achieving nothing and composing nothing. It wasn't supposed to be a jaunt around Europe on Daddy's credit, but Wolfgang had been away for a year and spent 863 gulden. Eventually his father and Baron von Grimm forcibly arranged his return to Salzburg. Leopold was worried sick when Wolfgang didn't arrive at his next stop — fearing that his son had been killed by highway robbers. He went absolutely bonkers when he discovered that Wolfgang was actually swanning around in Nancy, "playing ducks and drakes" with his father's money.

Your whole intention seems to be to ruin me, simply in order to go on building your castles in the air.

LEOPOLD MOZART TO WOLFGANG

It should have taken just twelve days until Wolfgang was embraced in Papa's loving arms again. But there was someone else Wolfgang wanted to embrace first — Aloysia Weber. He doodled and dallied his way home over four months, eventually tracking down Aloysia in Munich, where his beloved was now employed as soprano for a thousand gulden a year! Their reunion was a heart-wrenching affair … at least for Wolfgang. According to one of Mozart's early biographers, Aloysia pretended not to recognise her love-sick swain. Stung to the core, Wolfgang leapt on the nearest piano and began singing "Let the wench who doesn't want me kiss my ass".

SALZBURG

If the people of Salzburg want to have me, then they must meet all my wishes.

WOLFGANG

He was talking tough, but in January 1779 Wolfgang went crawling back to Salzburg's Prince-Archbishop Colloredo, with his tail between his legs. The twenty-three-year-old was adamant that he would only return if he was appointed the top job of court composer. In the end he took the position of court organist and a salary of 450 gulden — the same position he'd turned down at Versailles, but for only a quarter of the pay! It was the cruelest irony that, after a year of seeking employment amongst the leading nobles, Wolfgang accepted a job with the one aristocrat in Europe he detested the most.

The years '79 and '80 were spent confined to Salzburg. But there was still fun to be had with Papa and Nannerl. A favourite pastime for the family was air-gun shooting using feathered darts, and the old dance studio in their house made a perfect indoor range. Family and friends would take turns providing the elaborate targets for the shoot, which gives us another glimpse at the Mozart family's wacky sense of humour.

As for the shooting targets …
I would like you to paint this scene:
a short man with fair hair shown
bending over and displaying his bare ass.
From his mouth come the words:
"Bon appétit, have a good meal."

WOLFGANG

The Elector shouted Bravo … and said with a laugh: "Who would believe that such great things could be hidden in such a small head."

WOLFGANG

Towards the end of 1780, a stroke of luck came Wolfgang's way. Salzburg's court chaplain was asked to write the libretto for a new opera in Munich. Salzburg's Prince-Archbishop Colloredo couldn't turn down a double honour to his city, so allowed Wolfgang permission to travel to Munich to write the music for *Idomeneo*♪. Despite having "light brigades of slime and rot", due to a head cold, Wolfgang worked flat out for ten weeks, pulling out all his new ideas of how an opera should be. He cajoled and hassled the librettist, modernising the text, and improving the drama. Most importantly, Wolfgang introduced a brand-new idea — that the music should match each emotion of the text. Papa and Nannerl joined Wolfgang in Munich for the premier on his twenty-fifth birthday. They had a blast, enjoying the freedom away from Salzburg, and Wolfgang's small head was in serious danger of becoming swollen. With all the accolades from the nobility, would he be content to go back to Salzburg?

The Munich premier of Wolfgang's opera *Idomeneo* turned into an extended holiday with Papa and Nannerl. But the happy days couldn't last. In March 1781 Wolfgang was called to Vienna, where the Prince-Archbishop Colloredo was visiting his ailing father. Wolfgang was already spoiling for a fight during the interminable coach ride and, on arrival, the contrast in his status was made quite clear. He was in a highly sarcastic mood at being brought to heel amongst the crude servants of the archbishop's retinue.

The two valets sit at the top of the table, but at least I have the honour of being placed above the cooks ... I almost believe myself back in Salzburg!

WOLFGANG

89

Today we had a concert … which I composed
last night between 11 and 12. But in order
to complete it in time I wrote out just the violin
part … and kept my own part in my head.

WOLFGANG

In Salzburg I long for a hundred
amusements, but here, not a single one.
Just to be in Vienna is entertainment enough.

WOLFGANG

Previously, Wolfgang had sent his father coded letters in the fear that they were censored by the archbishop. Now he gave up hiding his feelings, calling the archbishop "ass", "mufti", "fool", "misanthrope" and "oaf" — actively courting antagonism. Wolfgang was champing at the bit to get out there in Vienna, but the archbishop just tightened his control. Wolfgang was there to serve the archbishop alone. Because of this, Wolfgang missed out on playing for the emperor and earning a substantial 250 gulden from one concert — half a year's salary! Instead he was ordered to compose and play new works on the spot for an unappreciative lord♪. Wolfgang could do that. The question was whether he wanted to any more, and a crazy idea began to form in his mind. He could be his own master. Something entirely new — a freelance composer.

I should not hesitate for a moment to quit the archbishop's service, give a grand concert and take on four pupils.

WOLFGANG

I am no longer so unfortunate to be in the service of Salzburg — today is that happy day for me … He called me a rascal and a dissolute fellow … and told me to "get out" that very instant.

WOLFGANG

The whole relationship between Wolfgang and his lord the archbishop came to a head at the start of May 1781. Wolfgang was ordered to take the next carriage home to Salzburg with some of the other servants, but the headstrong composer wanted to stay in wonderful Vienna. Wolfgang had actually managed to sneak in a few performances and he told the archbishop that he would stay a while to round up the takings. It was like a red rag to a bull, and this time the archbishop completely lost his cool.

Is it any wonder then …
I took his "get out" quite literally?

WOLFGANG

You allow yourself to be far too easily dazzled in Vienna. A man's fame here is short-lived … after a few months the Viennese will want something new.

COUNT ARCO TO WOLFGANG

Leopold Mozart joined forces with Count Arco (the archbishop's right-hand man in Vienna). They urged Wolfgang to play it safe, make nice and come back to his job in Salzburg. This time Wolfgang was done with crawling back to Salzburg, telling his father that he'd rather be a beggar than go on serving the archbishop.

Ask me what you will, only not to return to the archbishop. The mere thought makes me tremble with rage.

WOLFGANG

It is the heart that enobles a man.
Although I am not a count,
I probably have more honour
in me than many a count.

WOLFGANG

A servant simply did not leave his lord's service. It carried the threat of imprisonment or flogging. Before things came to blows, a war of gossip waged between the archbishop, Count Arco and Wolfgang, which was reported as far away as Augsburg. In the end, Count Arco refused Wolfgang permission to quit, but Wolfgang felt honour bound to stick to his guns. He'd been dreaming of this moment for years and he wasn't going to let it slip away now he was in Vienna. At the last minute, knowing they were losing their young genius, Count Arco lost his rag and quite literally gave Wolfgang a now famous "kick up the ass".

Let people write until their eyes pop out …
But I shall not alter by a hair's breadth;
I shall remain the same honest fellow as ever.

WOLFGANG

By the middle of 1781, the gossip had moved from Wolfgang's feud with the archbishop to his love life. He'd found a room in Vienna, staying with his old friends, the Weber family, who had moved to Vienna after the death of Herr Weber. Wolfgang's first love, Aloysia, was now a famous singer at the Vienna opera house. Meanwhile, back in Salzburg, Leopold was hearing rumours from all over the place — mainly that Wolfgang was getting far too friendly with one of Aloysia's younger sisters.

If I had to marry every lady
with whom I have jested, I should
have collected 200 wives by now.

WOLFGANG

Wolfgang set about making his way in Vienna with gusto, but he couldn't seem to shake those wedding rumours. He soon landed himself a remarkably talented pupil, Josepha Auernhammer. He dedicated a set of sonatas to her, and they performed one of his challenging piano ducts in concert♪. Their lessons came to a dramatic end when Wolfgang heard that they were getting married, and honeymooning in Italy — a rumour which Josepha herself had spread! With his wicked eye for characterisation, Wolfgang paints a cruelly evocative description of his love-sick pupil.

If an artist wanted to paint the devil as lifelike as possible, he would choose her face; she … sweats to make you sick, and dresses so scantily that one can read the message clearly: "Pray, look right here!" True, there's plenty to see, enough to strike you blind.

WOLFGANG

Vienna glowed in the summer of '81. Wolfgang was in a joyous mood and wrote one of his sweetest serenades♪. He was having the time of his life — joking around with his land lady's daughters, Constanze and Sophie Weber. Aside from the joking, he worked hard to impress the powers that be and was rewarded with a big opera commission. Wolfgang set about bringing his new emotional music to the Viennese with *The Abduction from the Seraglio*. What made it even more exciting was that this opera was to be in German, and Wolfgang was going to prove that his German opera was greater than all those frivolous Italian imports. He'd also discovered the music of Handel and J. S. Bach and became obsessed with absorbing the ideas of these old masters. Leopold Mozart tried hard to stay part of his son's career, sticking his oar in and offering his old point-by-point criticisms of everything Wolfgang was doing. This was all "nothing more than well-intentioned advice", replied Wolfgang. He was the master of his own destiny. As an artist, and as a young man, Wolfgang no longer sought any counsel.

I don't ask for anybody's advice or criticism … I simply follow my own feelings.

WOLFGANG

♪ SERENADE NO. 10 FOR WINDS IN B FLAT, K. 361

Can you believe it, but yesterday there was an even stronger cabal against my opera than on the first night! Throughout the first act people were hissing – but they couldn't drown out the loud shouts of "Bravo".

WOLFGANG

Wolfgang was always up against jealous cabals plotting to stop his success, and court composer Antonio Salieri was his main suspect as ringleader. This legendary rivalry would continue for the rest of Wolfgang's life. But despite the cabals, *The Abduction from the Seraglio* was a great success when it opened in the summer of 1782. Famously, Emperor Joseph II is supposed to have criticised the opera's "monstrous many notes", but *Seraglio* would go on to become Wolfgang's most popular opera during his lifetime. It's fascinating that Wolfgang reports the Viennese audience reacting throughout the opera. Leopold Mozart was thrilled – perhaps his son was going to succeed after all. Just as long as he didn't complicate things or burden himself with a wife …

I cannot think of anything more necessary to me than a wife … a bachelor is only half alive.

WOLFGANG

During the writing of *The Abduction from the Seraglio*, Wolfgang had slowly fallen in love with Constanze Weber. The young bachelor was embattled on all fronts — and not just from the cabals trying to bring down his opera. His father still blamed "those Webers" for everything that had gone wrong on Wolfgang's disastrous Paris adventure, and Stanzie's mother tried her best to keep the two lovers apart. It was a real soap opera, and Wolfgang sometimes mixed up reality and stage — confusing his new love, Constanze Weber, with Konstanze, the heroine in his opera, who must be rescued from the evil harem.

Constanze Weber

I am longing to set her free and to rescue her as soon as possible.

WOLFGANG

My beloved Konstanze; — she is not ugly, but at the same time not really beautiful; — her whole beauty consists of two little black eyes and a pretty figure … I love her and she loves me with all her heart. Tell me whether I could wish for a better wife?

WOLFGANG

This seems like a rather unflattering portrait of Wolfgang's beloved. However, it was a description intended to convince his father of Constanze's wifely virtues. Wolfgang is exaggerating the point that she's not just some pretty girl he's marrying for looks. It was all in hopes of mending the divisions which had grown between father, son and the future in-laws. The wedding was set for August 1782 in Vienna's St Stephen's Cathedral, and the couple waited and waited for a blessing from Leopold …

Stephansdom

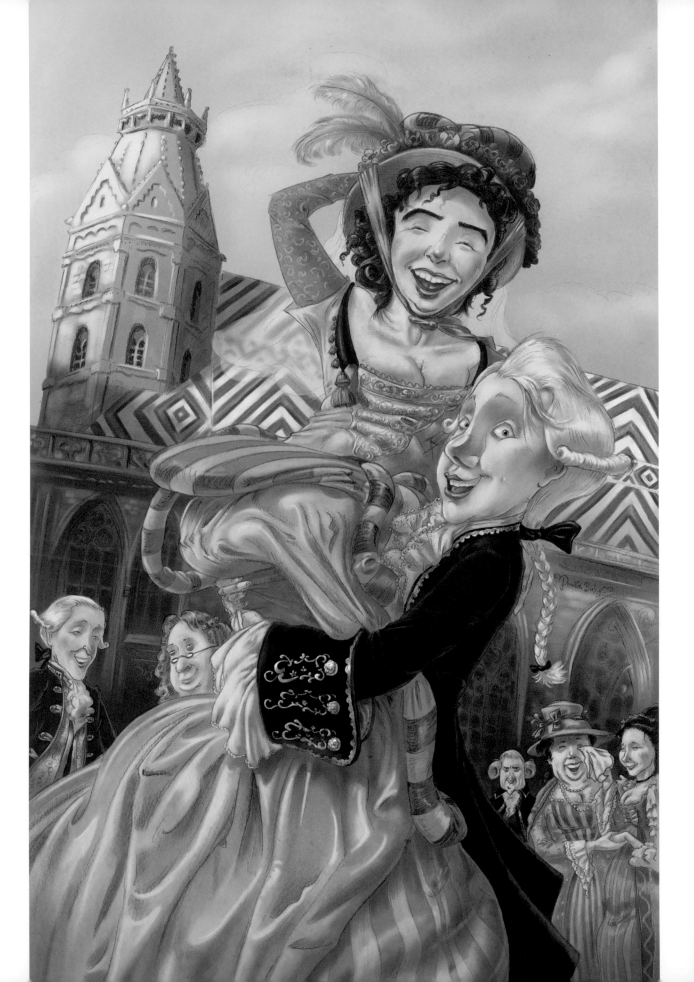

When we had been joined together, my wife and I began to weep — everybody was moved by that.

WOLFGANG

Constanze and Wolfgang became Frau and Herr Mozart on 4 August 1782. The wedding was a small ceremony with only a few witnesses, including Constanze's mother and younger sister, Sophie. An old childhood friend, Franz Gilowsky, now a surgeon in Vienna, was Wolfgang's best man. But the marriage had divided Wolfgang from the Salzburg Mozarts, and Leopold's blessing didn't arrive until after the wedding. Wolfgang's sister scornfully commented that her brother would always need someone to mother him. The artist *did* depend on someone to ground him, and Constanze was his rock. By spring the following year, the happy pair were about to become three.

My only company consists of my little wife who is pregnant, and hers consists of her little husband, who isn't pregnant, but fat and happy.

WOLFGANG

My dear wife was safely delivered of a fine, healthy boy, round as a butterball.

WOLFGANG

Wolfgang and Constanze's first child was born on 17 June 1783. "He's the spitting image of me," beamed the proud father. They had *intended* to call the baby Leopold or Leopoldina, but things turned out differently when Wolfgang's friend, and landlord, Baron Raimund Wetzlar, turned up and said, "Now you have a little Raimund."

The new parents decided to make a visit to Papa and Nannerl in Salzburg, while little Raimund remained in Vienna with a wet nurse. In Salzburg, Wolfgang's "Great Mass" was first performed♪. Prior to moving to Vienna, he had composed huge amounts of church music, but this one was a personal masterpiece. He'd written it for Constanze, when she had been seriously ill before their marriage, and in this first performance, she sung the soprano part. They wanted Leopold and Nannerl to see that she was a worthy musical companion for Wolfgang. Beyond the strained family dynamics was Wolfgang's unresolved split from Salzburg's Prince-Archbishop. Wolfgang was worried that he would be arrested at any moment. Thankfully, that threat was the least of their worries, but a genuine tragedy awaited their return to Vienna. Their precious little butterball had died.

Your son is the greatest composer known to me either in person or by name. He has taste and, what is more, the most profound knowledge of composition.

JOSEPH HAYDN TO LEOPOLD MOZART

The golden years began in 1784. Wolfgang had become hugely popular in Vienna, and in March alone he gave eighteen concerts. In the following month he wrote "the best work I have ever composed"♪. He was on fire — performing ad lib at a concert before the emperor, and there was so much demand from his fans that the next few years were a whirlwind of creativity. Leopold Mozart had heard the rumours, but when he visited Vienna in February '85 he saw his son's true success. The tables were overflowing with masses of new works, including two piano concertos which would become his most famous♪. The movers were constantly taking Wolfgang's precious piano to performances and Wolfgang had thousands of gulden in the bank. The accolade from Joseph Haydn must have been the icing on the cake.

♪ QUINTET IN E FLAT MAJOR FOR PIANO AND WINDS, K. 452
PIANO CONCERTO NO. 20 IN D MINOR, K. 466
PIANO CONCERTO NO. 21 IN C MAJOR, K. 467

These happy years welcomed a new home and a new baby. Carl was born on 21 September 1784, and the young family moved into a beautiful apartment in the heart of Vienna, now known as The Figarohaus. Baby Carl survived the dangerous first eighteen months, and with the toddler making mischief around the house, Wolfgang began writing his next great masterpiece, *The Marriage of Figaro*♪.

The greatness of his genius demanded a subject which should be ample, elevated and abounding in character and incident.

LORENZO DA PONTE ON MOZART

*F*igaro was certainly abounding in incident! It was the first time audiences had seen a contemporary setting and realistic characters in an opera. Wolfgang joined forces with librettist Lorenzo Da Ponte to create a revolutionary work — where servants stood up against their masters — a subject which greatly appealed to Wolfgang! Add to this Mozart's astounding music, which conveys every nuance and emotion perfectly. *Figaro* was so different, that it was originally billed as "virtually a new kind of play". Wolfgang's genius was to create a work which instantly appeals to the everyday listener, yet contains incredible complexities that only the connoisseur can appreciate. As usual, tremendous cabals worked to prevent Wolfgang's success, and *Figaro*'s first run, in May 1786, lasted only nine performances. Today, *Figaro*'s themes of social equality are just as beautiful and powerful as when they were first written, and it remains one of the most popular operas of all time.

FIGAROHAUS

Wolfgang and Stanzie's third child arrived in October 1786, but with the failure of *Figaro*, they were seriously considering departing Vienna. Wolfgang tried to get Papa to take care of two-year-old Carl and new-born Johann, so he and Stanzie could relocate to London — but Leopold was already looking after Nannerl's son. The plan was soon abandoned when Johann died less than a month later. Wolfgang slipped into despondence, but good news came from afar. In January 1787 he was invited to conduct *Figaro* in Prague, where the city had gone hopping mad for Mozart's music. He was immediately commissioned to write a new opera, and he returned to Vienna to work on *Don Giovanni*.

Everyone was hopping about with sheer delight to the music of my "Figaro" … nothing is played, blown, sung or whistled but "Figaro".

WOLFGANG

Keep your eyes on him; some day he will give the world something to talk about.

WOLFGANG ON HEARING BEETHOVEN PLAY

In April 1787, a young musician from Bonn arrived in Vienna. The sixteen-year-old had been proclaimed as "a second Wolfgang Amadeus Mozart" by his first teacher, and now sought lessons from the maestro himself. According to the story, thirty-one-year-old Wolfgang was initially unimpressed when young Ludwig van Beethoven played a party piece from memory. Wolfgang's indifference soon turned to amazement when the teenager launched into an improvisation. Wolfgang's teaching style was very strong on rhythm, improvisation and sight reading and, contrary to the above anecdote, Wolfgang was amazed at students who could play from memory. These two musical giants spent two weeks together, before Beethoven returned to Bonn when his mother became ill.

I never lie down at night without reflecting that, young as I am, I may not live to see another day. Yet none of my friends would say that I am morose.

WOLFGANG

Death was on Wolfgang's mind in 1787. A friend his own age had died, and in May, Leopold Mozart passed away. Leopold had been a controlling papa — at times niggly and negative towards Wolfgang's plans — but he had sacrificed everything for his son's success. In fact, Leopold had made Wolfgang the genius he was. Wolfgang's last letter to his father is filled with philosophical musings on life and death, and is a stark contrast to the helplessness that he felt when his mother passed away. Wolfgang tried to shake off any dark thoughts with his usual light-hearted spirit, even staging a mock funeral for his pet bird. He was unable to attend Leopold's funeral, and instead poured all these emotions into a new opera, combining death and humour in his dark comedy, *Don Giovanni.*

Death, when we consider it closely, is the true goal of our existence … his image is no longer terrifying to me.

WOLFGANG

Wolfgang embraced his complex feelings in *Don Giovanni*, a strange new opera. Comedy and drama join forces on stage, ending when the lustful Don is dragged into the fires of hell, accompanied by a rich, swirling torrent of music. Many critics have called *Don Giovanni* the greatest opera ever written. However, at the time, it was a bit *too* strange and new for the Viennese audiences. Once again, though, the city of Prague embraced Wolfgang's opera, and *Don Giovanni* premiered on 29 October 1787 in Prague's Estates Theatre — the only theatre still existing where Mozart worked in his lifetime.

Wolfgang owned several birds throughout his life, from tomtits and robins in his childhood to the canary which shared his room during his final days. Vogel Star was a starling which Wolfgang had bought at the market in 1784. Starlings are remarkable mimics and Wolfgang recorded that Vogel Star sung the opening bars to a piano concerto he was writing♪.

Other pets included Miss Pimperl, a fox terrier the Mozarts owned in Salzburg, and Wolfgang and Constanze had at least two dogs in Vienna. In his final years, Wolfgang bought a horse and took up riding on doctor's orders — a health fix which didn't last long.

The quote on the opposite page is a literal translation of Wolfgang's heart-felt, yet comedic, rhyme written when Vogel Star died in June 1787, only a few days after Leopold Mozart's death. Wolfgang staged a mock funeral for Vogel Star, and perhaps the playful ceremony was a way to deal with the loss of his father.

Here lies a dear fool, a starling bird.

Even in the prime of life,

he experienced the bitter pain of death.

My heart bleeds when I remember it.

O dear reader! Howl for him, too.

WOLFGANG ON HIS BIRD VOGEL STAR

*D*on Giovanni brought Wolfgang some much needed money, and the birth of daughter Theresia in December 1787 was another good sign. That light-hearted spirit shines through in his famous *Eine kleine nachtmusik♪*, written during this testing year. But Wolfgang's next few years were to prove far more stressful. He was still thinking of quitting Vienna, and in a cunning move, he let this gossip be known to the newspapers. The palace took the bait, and at the age of thirty-two he finally received that elusive court position he'd been aiming for his entire life.

The Mozarts had always been a little behind the creditors, but now their struggles came in waves. Wolfgang's new salary had to be eeked out between six-monthly instalments, and with Stanzie's endless pregnancies came endless illnesses and endless bills, Wolfgang was working every hour to earn money, manage the household and look after his wife, yet he was making no headway. Things were compounded when Theresia died in June 1788. Wolfgang was beset by "black thoughts" and soon after wrote his haunting *Symphony No. 40♪*. That same month, the deeply depressed composer began a long series of letters, begging for money from his shrinking circle of friends.

O God! – I can hardly bring myself to despatch this letter … to beg so shamelessly from my only friend.

WOLFGANG

After several wobbly years, 1791 was shaping up to be Wolfgang's steady comeback. He was working on *The Magic Flute*, a thrilling new opera that would be something quite different. However, Wolfgang *wasn't* thrilled to have second billing behind Emanuel Schikaneder — the opera's writer, director and star. Wolfgang would get Schikaneder back with a little joke later on. Meanwhile Constanze and Carl were staying in Baden, a health spa just south of Vienna, where Constanze was expecting her sixth child (after losing baby Anna Maria soon after birth in November 1789). Wolfgang visited as often as he could. He was in a sweet mood, and wrote his angelic *Ave Verum Corpus*♪ for the choirmaster he befriended in the spa town.

Catch—bis—bis—bs—bs—lots of little kisses are flying about for you — bs — why, here's another one, wobbling after the rest.

WOLFGANG

Wolfgang longed to be with Carl and Stanzie in Baden, but they had to be content with his flying kisses. Wolfgang was forced to stay in Vienna, because in the middle of writing *The Magic Flute* came two big commissions — one for a requiem mass, then a second opera, for Emperor Leopold II's coronation. Writing two operas in a matter of months was a staggering task but Wolfgang took it all on. After the last few years, he wasn't about to turn down any work. Besides, he had a family of four to support now. On 26 July 1791, Constanze gave birth to Xaver, their second surviving son.

Salieri listened and watched most attentively and from the overture to the last chorus there was not a single number that did not call forth from him a bravo! or bello!

WOLFGANG

*T*he *Magic Flute* ♪ was a popular smash when it opened in September 1791. It didn't play in the grand Italian opera houses — but in the suburbs, sung in plain German. Its sets and special effects cost a staggering 5000 gulden and included a very contemporary hot-air balloon and a gigantic snake. Wolfgang took his mother-in-law Frau Weber, seven-year-old Carl, and his off-and-on rival Salieri to see it from his personal box. Salieri cheered, and Carl was enthralled. Mozart's music is often described in dynamic contrasts of childlike and genius — so simple that any child could play it, yet incredibly difficult for professional performers. *The Magic Flute* was sublime complexity, a blockbuster fit for the greatest connoisseurs and the child at heart.

As *The Magic Flute* went from strength to strength, Wolfgang cheerfully reported the audience approval. They especially liked the, now famous, glockenspiel aria sung by Papageno♪. The part was played by the star of the show, Emanuel Schikaneder, but the glockenspiel was actually performed by an orchestra member off-stage. Wolfgang was in a happy trickster mood when he decided to play a joke on Schikaneder, and let the audience in on the secret.

During Papageno's aria I went behind the scenes. I had an impulse to play the glockenspiel myself for a laugh … when Schikaneder came to a pause, I played an arpeggio. He was startled … he struck the glockenspiel and said "shut up!" Everybody laughed … many learning for the first time that Papegeno doesn't play the instrument himself.

WOLFGANG

Carl was absolutely delighted at being taken to the opera … his school is probably fine for turning out a good peasant into the world! … he still has his old bad manners … enjoys learning *even less* because all he does is wander about the garden, for 5 hours in the morning and 5 hours in the afternoon.

WOLFGANG

As 1791 came to a close, the Mozart family were looking to the future. Stanzie was on the mend, little Xaver was doing well, and Wolfgang was taking an active interest in Carl's schooling. After visiting Carl's headmaster, Wolfgang decided to send his son to an expensive boarding school that would cost 400 gulden per year — almost as much as his old salary back in Salzburg. The family's fortunes were on the rise.

Did I not say that I was writing this Requiem for myself?

WOLFGANG

As a child, Wolfgang had almost died on the European tours from typhoid and smallpox, and his overall health had been seriously weakened by many illnesses throughout his life. Through November 1791, Wolfgang became sicker and sicker, but he still had a grand requiem mass to complete♪. According to one of his first biographers, Wolfgang prophetically stated that the requiem would be for his own funeral. This final work would stand as one of his greatest masterpieces and is often shrouded in myth because it was commissioned by a mysterious stranger. Years later, in a lawsuit over ownership, Constanze uncovered the anonymous stranger as Count Franz von Walsegg-Stuppach, an aristocrat and amateur composer, who liked to pass off compositions as his own.

The first few days of December 1791 started well, and Wolfgang felt good enough to get out and about. Then on 4 December his health took a dramatic dive. Family and friends gathered at his bedside, and Wolfgang's sister-in-law, Sophie, later recalled the whole event for one of Mozart's early biographers. Carl remembered his father in an awful state, swollen and paralysed on one side. Still Wolfgang struggled to finish his requiem, dictating to one of his pupils how it should be completed. When the doctor eventually turned up, his remedies only made matters worse, throwing Wolfgang into a coma. He passed away just before one o'clock the next morning. He was only thirty-five.

His last movement was an attempt
to express with his mouth the drum
passage in the Requiem.

SOPHIE, MOZART'S SISTER-IN-LAW

In the presence of God,
the angels all play Bach.
But when they are alone,
I am sure they play Mozart.

KARL BARTH

Afterword

Wolfgang Amadeus Mozart died in the early hours of Monday, 5 December 1791. He had been seriously weakened by severe illnesses throughout his life, and his death was most likely brought on by a combination of long-term ailments, including kidney failure.

After a private service at St Stephen's Cathedral in Vienna, his body was taken to the cemetery of St Marx where he was buried without ceremony in an unmarked grave. This was not because Mozart was a pauper; rather, reforms had been passed to make Vienna's overcrowded graveyards more efficient and hygienic. Common graves were dug over every decade to make room for new burials — the practice robbing Mozart of a permanent resting place. The cemetery was six kilometres out of town, so only a handful of people attended the actual burial, including Mozart's long-time rival, Antonio Salieri.

1791 had actually been one of Mozart's most successful years, but as a freelance artist his income fluctuated wildly, and the Mozarts had no provision for the future. At just twenty-nine, Constanze was left to provide for herself and her two sons. It was in their best interests to preserve her husband's legacy, and she personally oversaw the publication of Mozart's works. In 1809 Constanze married the Danish diplomat Georg Nikolaus von Nissen, who, with Constanze's help, wrote one of the first in-depth biographies of Mozart.

Wolfgang and Constanze's son Carl did not inherit his father's musical talents; however his younger brother, Xaver, went on to become a fine concert pianist, even changing his name to Wolfgang. But as George Bernard Shaw noted: "How could any man do what was expected from Mozart's son? Not Mozart himself even."

Mozart had broken hard ground as an independent composer, leading new innovations in the popular style, symphony, church music and especially opera. He paved the way for composers to be respected as artists in their own right. At the time of his death, Mozart was far from the romantic image of the unmourned genius. In Prague alone four thousand people attended his memorial service. Fittingly, his unfinished Requiem Mass was performed for the first time at a service marking his death.

On hearing of the passing of his young friend, Joseph Haydn said, "Posterity will not have such a talent again in one hundred years." He might as well have said one thousand.

Timeline

1756
Salzburg, 27 January. Johannes Chrysostomus Wolfgangus Theophilus Sigismundus Mozart is born to Anna Maria and Leopold Mozart. He is the last of seven children and only the second to survive.

1760 AGE 4
Wolfgang's eight-year-old sister, Nannerl, begins to learn the harpsichord.

1761 AGE 5
Wolfgang begins writing his first compositions by finding notes on the keyboard that "like each other".

1762 AGE 6
In January, Leopold takes his two gifted children for their first big performance in Munich. In September they are invited to the Imperial Palace in Vienna, where Wolfgang proposes to the child Archduchess Marie Antoinette.

1777 AGE 21
Wolfgang resigns his job in Salzburg. In September he sets off with his mother to secure a better position at one of the Southern German Courts.

1778 AGE 22
In Mannheim, Wolfgang falls in love with a young singer, Aloysia Weber. Leopold orders his son and wife on to Paris, where Wolfgang composes his great "Paris" Symphony (No. 31), and his sublime concerto for flute and harp.

1778 AGE 22
Just when things are looking up for Wolfgang in Paris, his mother, Anna Maria, dies on 3 July.

1779 AGE 23
Aloysia Weber rejects Wolfgang's affections and he returns home to Salzburg, begrudgingly accepting the position of court organist.

1781 AGE 25
Wolfgang quits the Salzburg court orchestra once and for all, and settles in Vienna as a freelance composer. He stays with his old friends, the Weber family, who are now resident in the city, where he slowly falls in love with Constanze Weber, Aloysia's younger sister.

1782 AGE 26
Wolfgang and Constanze Weber are married at St Stephen's Cathedral in Vienna on 4 August.

1784-85 AGE 29
These are Wolfgang's most successful years, with endless concerts and acclaim from both the public and fellow composers. In February and March 1785, Wolfgang composes his great piano concertos, Nos. 20, 21 and 22.

1783 AGE 27
On 17 June Wolfgang and Constanze's first child, Raimund Leopold, is born. The couple visit Leopold and Nannerl in Salzburg, where Wolfgang's "Great Mass" in C minor is first performed. On returning to Vienna they discover that little Raimund has died.

1784 AGE 28
On 21 September Wolfgang and Constanze's second child, Carl Thomas, is born.

1786 AGE 30
The masterpieces continue to come when Wolfgang premieres *The Marriage of Figaro* in Vienna. This innovative opera is "virtually a new kind of play" and although not initially successful, it will go on to be considered one of the greatest operas ever written.

SALZBURG

1763 AGE 7
Leopold decides to take the whole family on a grand tour of Europe and England.

1764 AGE 8
In London, Leopold Mozart falls ill and eight-year-old Wolfgang finds something quiet to do by composing his first symphony.

1766 AGE 10
In November 1766, the Mozarts finally return home to Salzburg after almost three and a half years on tour.

1768 AGE 12
Wolfgang writes *La Finta Semplice*, his first opera (a genre that he will one day make his own).

1769 AGE 13
Wolfgang gets his first appointment (although without pay) as violinist and Third Konzertmeister in the Salzburg court orchestra.

1773 AGE 17
Leopold and Wolfgang travel to Vienna in an unsuccessful attempt to secure Wolfgang a position at the Imperial Court. Back in Salzburg Wolfgang composes his first great Symphony, No. 25.

1770 AGE 14
In Rome Pope Clement XIV makes Wolfgang a knight of the Order of the Golden Spur. The honours continue in Bologna, where Wolfgang is accepted as the youngest maestro at the famous Accademia Filarmonica.

1769 AGE 13
In December, Leopold and Wolfgang set out on an Italian tour, the first of three they will undertake between 1770 and 1772.

Wolfgang Mozart

1787 AGE 31
In April, sixteen-year-old Ludwig van Beethoven arrives in Vienna to take lessons with Mozart. On 28 May, Wolfgang's father, Leopold Mozart, dies.

1787 AGE 31
After a lifetime of seeking a secure position at court, Wolfgang is finally awarded the part-time position of "Imperial Chamber Music Composer" in Vienna.

1788 AGE 32
With health and financial problems, Wolfgang is "beset ... frequently by black thoughts". In summer he composes his three last symphonies; they include his haunting masterpiece, symphony No. 40.

1789 AGE 33
Health problems continue for both Wolfgang and Constanze. To compound matters, war with the Turks reduces demand for Wolfgang's concerts, leading him to write a series of begging letters to his friends.

1791 AGE 35
In late November Wolfgang's health takes a sudden dive and he works feverishly to complete a commission for a Requiem Mass.

1791 AGE 35
Wolfgang works on his last opera, *The Magic Flute*. Its premiere in September is a tremendous success and it will go on to be one of his enduring masterpieces.

1791 AGE 35
On 26 July, Wolfgang and Constanze's last child, Franz Xaver is born. He is only the second of six to survive beyond infancy.

1791 AGE 35
In the early hours of 5 December, Wolfgang Amadeus Mozart dies.

About the author

Donovan Bixley is one of New Zealand's most acclaimed picture-book creators with over one hundred books published in thirty-one countries. His books have been twice selected for the International Youth Library's White Raven, and his numerous awards include the Mallinson Rendel Illustrators Award and the Russell Clark Illustration Award.

Donovan first discovered Mozart's letters twenty years ago, and was inspired to create *Faithfully Mozart*, a six-year labour of love, which was published internationally in 2005. After the success of Donovan's illustrated biography, *Much Ado About Shakespeare*, he wanted to re-format *Faithfully Mozart* in the same easy, engaging style. The resulting book, *Mozart – The Man Behind the Music*, incorporates artwork from the original book as well as new material, illuminating the wider world of this fascinating genius.

When not immersed in the world of picture books, Donovan plays saxophone, and is singer for a thirteen-piece jazz/funk band, Hot Tub. He lives with his family in Taupo, New Zealand.

A catalogue record for this book is available
from the National Library of New Zealand

ISBN 978-1-988516-19-6

An Upstart Press Book
Published in 2018 by Upstart Press Ltd
Level 4, 15 Huron Street, Takapuna 0622
Auckland, New Zealand

Printed by 1010 Printing International Ltd., China